GREAT PICTURES

AND THEIR STORIES

How To Look At Pictures

"You must look at pictures studiously, earnestly, honestly. It will take years before you come to a full appreciation of art; but when at last you have it, you will be possessed of the purest, loftiest and most ennobling pleasures that the civilized world can offer you."

JOHN C. VAN DYKE.

ST.
AA
PRESS

GREAT PICTURES
AND THEIR STORIES

INTERPRETING
MASTERPIECES
TO CHILDREN

BY
KATHERINE MORRIS LESTER

BOOK ONE

ST. AUGUSTINE ACADEMY PRESS

This book was originally published in 1927
by Mentzer, Bush & Company.

This facsimile edition reprinted in 2024
with improved color images
by St. Augustine Academy Press.

ISBN: 978-1-64051-144-6

CONTENTS

Page

Baby Stuart ....*Van Dyck* 17

Nurse and Child.............*Hals* 21

The Calmady Children.......*Lawrence* 29

Madonna of the Chair........*Raphael* 35

With Grandma...............*MacEwen* 42

Children of the Shell..........*Murillo* 51

Princess Margarita Theresa...*Velasquez* 58

Feeding Her Birds...........*Millet* 66

Children of the Sea...........*Israels* 74

Holy Night..................*Correggio* 83

INDEX OF ILLUSTRATIONS IN GREAT PICTURES AND THEIR STORIES

BOOK ONE—FIRST GRADE
(All in Color) Page
1. Baby Stuart................17
2. Nurse and Child...........21
3. The Calmady Children......29
4. Madonna of the Chair......35
5. With Grandma.............42
6. Children of the Shell......51
7. Princess Margarita Theresia..58
8. Feeding her Birds..........66
9. Children of the Sea........74
10. The Holy Night............83

BOOK TWO—SECOND GRADE
(All in Color) Page
1. A Holiday.................13
2. Mme. Lebrun and Her
    Daughter...............21
3. Don Carlos on Horseback....28
4. The Boy With a Rabbit......37
5. The Storage Room.........45
6. The Pastry Eaters.........53
7. The Age of Innocence.......61
8. Home Work................69
9. Children of Charles I.......77
10. Sistine Madonna...........84

BOOK THREE—THIRD GRADE
(All in Color) Page
1. Miss Bowles................13
2. Hearing...................20
3. Dancing in a Ring..........29
4. Angel With a Lute.........37
5. An Aristocrat..............45
6. Carnation, Lily, Lily, Rose...53
7. Return to the Fold.........61
8. Pilgrims Going to Church....69
9. Going to Church, Moravia....77
10. The Primitive Sculptor......85

BOOK FOUR—FOURTH GRADE
(All in Color) Page
1. Aurora.....................13
2. The Horse Fair.............25
3. Behind the Plow............35
4. Venetian Waters............47
5. The Sheepfold..............59
6. The Gleaners...............69
7. The Solemn Pledge.........81
8. Preparing for Church........93
9. Going to Market...........103
10. The Blue Boy.............115

BOOK FIVE—FIFTH GRADE
(9 in Color—Statue in Black) Page
1. Spring Dance...............13
2. After a Summer Shower......25
3. The Sewing School..........33
4. Russian Winter............41
5. Return of the Fishermen....49
6. Song of the Lark...........61
7. Santa Fe Trail.............72
8. Appeal to the Great Spirit....81
9. Lady With a Lute..........93
10. Galahad the Deliverer.....105

BOOK SIX—SIXTH GRADE
(9 in Color—Statue in Black) Page
1. The Jester.................13
2. The Mill..................21
3. A Flower Girl of Holland.....33
4. View of Ghent.............45
5. A Dutch Interior...........53
6. The Fog Warning...........65
7. Joan of Arc...............73
8. Joan of Arc...............85
9. Christ in the Temple.......93
10. The Angelus..............105

BOOK SEVEN—SEVENTH GRADE
(9 in Color—Statue in Black) Page
1. Moonlight, Wood's Island
    Light...................13
2. Sir Galahad...............25
3. The Vigil.................37
4. Dance of the Nymphs.......45
5. Icebound..................57
6. The Concert...............65
7. King Cophetua and the
    Beggar Maid............77
8. Frieze of the Prophets (Detail) 89
9. Bartolomeo Colleoni........101
10. Avenue of Trees..........109

BOOK EIGHT—EIGHTH GRADE
(9 in Color—Statue in Black Page
1. George Washington.........13
2. On the Stairs..............25
3. Cotopaxi.................33
4. Syndics of the Cloth Guild....45
5. The Artist's Mother........57
6. Church at Old Lyme........69
7. The Last Supper...........77
8. St. Genevieve.............89
9. The Fighting Temeraire.....101
10. Victory of Samothrace.....113

BOOK NINE—FOR JR. AND SR. HIGH AND NORMAL SCHOOLS
Page
1. James Whitcomb Riley......10
2. The Mill Pond.............22
3. The Northeaster...........30
4. The Whistling Boy..........42
5. Men of the Docks..........54

Page
6. The Virgin.................66
7. King Lear.................78
8. Battersea Bridge..........90
9. The Apotheosis of Pittsburgh.102
10. Abraham Lincoln.......... 114

FOREWORD

Picture Study is rapidly becoming an important factor in our public school education. "Nearly every progressive city," says the Bureau of Education, Washington, D. C., "is making use of some form of picture study in the public school system."

The twentieth century has ushered in the reproduction of masterpieces in color! To what heights of delight the children of the Public Schools may be carried by the famous pictures of the world in color!

It remains only for the elders to choose pictures adapted to the childish interests; pictures which will cultivate a taste for the best in art; pictures which through the impressionable early years will lead to a true understanding and appreciation of the world's masterpieces!

In preparing this series of readers it has been the aim of those selecting the pictures to

11

consider always the child interest. The field of pictures is large. Not only have the "old masters" been drawn upon, but masters in modern art as well, including modern American artists. Thus constantly, through this series of pictures, the principles of beauty which made possible the "old masters" of yesterday are seen again in the art of today.

In the preparation of the text the child's interest and his ability to read are carefully considered. Real picture knowledge is conveyed in the child's own language.

In the primary grades the interest is largely in "what it is all about." Consequently the text aims to satisfy this curiosity, and at the same time lead to unconscious observation of those things which are most alive to the little child,—color, life, and action.

The vocabulary for Books I, II, and III is based on "The Reading Vocabulary,"* by Horn, Horn, and Packer.

*See twenty-fourth Year Book, National Society for the Study of Education; Part I, 1925.

In the intermediate grades, a lively interest in the story is always uppermost. Gradually an appreciation of picture-pattern develops. Simple elements in picture making,—i.e., center of interest, repetition of line and color,—may be intelligently comprehended by children of the intermediate grades.

In the grammar grades great interest in the story continues, and with this interest there develops an appreciation of HOW the story is told,—the real ART of the picture. The pupil not only learns that the picture is a masterpiece, but WHY. He thus acquires standards for judging other pictures.

Each picture is followed by a short sketch of the artist, told in a key adapted to the age and interest of the child.

The questions which follow the text will assist in developing an intelligent appreciation of the picture.

The author is particularly indebted to Miss Jennie Long, recently Supervisor of Primary

Education, Peoria Public Schools, for valuable criticism of the primary text. Grateful acknowledgment is also made for the opportunity of practical work with a selected number of primary stories in the schools of Peoria.

The manuscripts of the intermediate and grammar grade books have been submitted to teachers of those grades, to whom the author is indebted for helpful practical suggestions.

The MUSICAL RENDERINGS for the pictures have been graciously contributed by Eva G. Kidder, Director of Music, Peoria Public Schools. The author believes this to be a very valuable feature of these books.

KATHERINE MORRIS LESTER.

ILLUSTRATED WITH REPRO-
DUCTIONS IN COLOR FROM
THE ORIGINAL MASTER-
PIECES, BY COURTESY OF
THE ART EXTENSION
SOCIETY OF NEW YORK.

BABY STUART
Gallery St. Luca, Rome

ARTIST: Sir Anthony Van Dyck
SCHOOL: Flemish
DATES: 1599-1640

BABY STUART

Oh! What a pretty baby!
What a dear, pretty baby!
This is Baby Stuart.

Baby Stuart's father was a king.
His mother was a beautiful queen.
They were very proud
    of their beautiful baby.
"We must have a picture
    of our baby," said the queen.
"Yes!" said the king, "Baby Stuart
    must have his picture painted."

So the king called a great artist
    to the palace.
He asked him to paint the picture
    of the beautiful baby.

17

Soon Baby Stuart was dressed
   in his best clothes.
The artist gave him a red ball.
It was a big ball
   for his little hands.
He sat very still.
At last the picture was finished.
See the dear little baby head!
He has such a round face.
He has big, bright, beautiful eyes.
He has pretty little hands.
He wears his best bonnet.
It is tied under his chin.
His dress is blue silk.
It has big sleeves with cuffs
   of fine lace.
Baby, in his pretty dress,
   made a lovely picture
   for the king and queen.

THE STORY OF THE ARTIST

A great artist made this picture
  of Baby Stuart.
He painted Baby Stuart many times.
This is the picture
  that the king and queen
  liked best of all.
A beautiful baby
  makes a beautiful picture!

SOMETHING TO TELL

1. Have you ever had
    your picture taken?
2. Was Baby's picture made like yours?
3. What do you like best
    about Baby's picture?

Related Music: KING BABY....*H. Parker*
                        BABY DEAR .....*Huerter*

NURSE AND CHILD
Berlin Gallery

ARTIST: Frans Hals
SCHOOL: Dutch
DATES: 1580-1666

NURSE AND CHILD

Baby is having her picture painted!
She is very happy.
See her smile!

My! What a beautiful dress!
What a beautiful bonnet!
What beautiful lace collar and cuffs!

Is this a little American baby?
No, no! American babies do not wear
    such fine dresses!
They do not wear fine laces.

This is a little Dutch baby.
She has a little round face.
She has bright laughing eyes,
    and a funny little nose.

One day mother wanted a picture
of her baby.
So nurse dressed baby
in her best clothes.
She put on a very pretty dress
of golden brown.
She put on
her finest lace collar and cuffs.
She put a beautiful golden chain
around her neck.
"Baby looks very fine," said nurse,
"She will make a beautiful picture
for mother."

Nurse and baby went
to see the artist.
He was very happy.
"Yes, yes, said the artist,
"Baby will make a beautiful picture."

So nurse holds baby on her arm.
She spreads out her beautiful dress
   to show it off.
Baby stands in nurse's lap.
But she will not stand still!
She likes to laugh,
   and kick, and coo.
Nurse tries to keep her quiet.
She is holding up an apple.
Baby does not want the apple!
She wants only to watch the artist
   as he works.
She likes to see him
   make the pretty colors.
She thinks
   it's lots of fun.
Soon the artist began to talk.
He told funny stories
   as he worked.

Baby stood very, very still
as she listened.
Then the artist drew
her merry little face
and laughing eyes!
He drew her pretty lace collar
and cuffs.
He drew her wonderful dress.
Then he painted it
in beautiful colors.
Soon the picture was finished.

How mother liked the picture
of her little Dutch baby!
She liked the laughing eyes.
She liked the funny little nose.
She liked the beautiful dress.
She liked the picture
of the nurse, too.

Nurse is very happy
to have her picture painted
with the little Dutch baby.
She knows
that all the boys and girls
in all the world
will love the little Dutch baby.

Some day baby will grow
to be a very fine lady.
How she will smile
when she sees her baby picture
with her good kind nurse!

Baby and nurse have been smiling
out of this picture
for three hundred years.
Do you know
they are smiling at you?

THE STORY OF THE ARTIST

This artist lived in Holland
  by the sea.
He is a Dutch painter.
He is one of the great painters
  of the world.
He painted, "Nurse and Child"
  over three hundred years ago.
He always painted
  bright happy children.
He liked to paint
  fine clothes and pretty laces.
He liked best to paint
  happy smiles
  and laughing eyes.
No one could paint a smile
  better than he.
Now many people go to Holland
  to see his smiling faces.

SOMETHING TO TELL.

1. Where does baby live?
   Why is she dressed so fine?
   Why does she smile?

2. Name the colors in her dress.
   What does she wear
      around her neck?
   Where are the fine laces?

3. Who holds baby?
   Why does she smile?

4. Who is more important,
      nurse or baby?

5. What does this artist paint best?
   Why do you like baby's picture?

Related music: HUMORESQUE....*Dvorak*
                 BADINAGE ......*Herbert*

THE CALMADY CHILDREN
Metropolitan Museum, New York

ARTIST: Sir Thomas Lawrence
SCHOOL: English
DATES: 1769-1830

THE CALMADY CHILDREN

What a beautiful baby!

She is so happy and lively.

She likes
  to have her picture painted.

Sister smiles
  because baby is so happy.

Ho! Ho! This is just the picture
  the artist wanted!

He drew a big round circle.

He drew baby and sister
  side by side
  within the circle.

He made baby's arm with a curve
  like the circle.

He drew baby's sash with a curve
  like the circle.

Then he drew many curves
  within the circle!

Baby is standing
  in the big velvet chair.
She is so happy and lively!
Sister stands beside the chair.

See the baby's pretty little face!
She has two bright eyes.
See her pretty little mouth!
She has four white teeth.
She has pretty curls, too.
She has one little curl
  near each bright eye.
She has two little curls!

Sister is smiling, too.
She likes to see her baby sister
  full of life and fun!
She likes to see her baby sister
  dance and play!

See the pretty dresses!
They are soft and white.
Baby's dress is full of air.
It has many pretty curves.

Sister wears a blue sash.
It curves up like the circle.
She wears a little golden chain
  around her neck.
She has pretty brown curls, too.
She smiles and looks at baby
  as she dances
  in the big velvet chair.

The artist loved
  these two pretty children.
He knew they would make
  a beautiful picture
  in the big round circle!

THE STORY OF THE ARTIST

The artist painted this picture
of the Calmady children
over one hundred years ago.
What beautiful children lived
one hundred years ago!
This artist loved
to paint pictures of children.
He always painted
bright, happy faces.
He always used beautiful colors.
He thought the Calmady children
the most beautiful children
he had ever seen.
He was very happy
when he had finished the picture
of the two little girls.
He said,—
"This is my best picture."

SOMETHING TO TELL

1. Why is baby so lively?
   Why does sister smile?

2. What did the artist draw first?
   Can you find any curves
      in the picture?
   Why did the artist
      make the pretty curves?

3. What is the color
      of baby's dress?
   What is the color
      of sister's sash?
   What is the color
      of the chair?

4. How old is the picture?
   What did the artist say about it?

5. What do you like best about it?

MADONNA OF THE CHAIR
Pitti Palace, Florence

ARTIST: Raphael Sanzio
SCHOOL: Italian
DATES: 1483-1520

MADONNA OF THE CHAIR

What a beautiful mother and baby!
How the baby loves his mother!
The mother loves the baby, too!

This is the picture
   of the child, Jesus,
   and his mother.
The little boy standing near
   is his good friend.
His name is John.

One day the artist was walking
   in the country.
He saw the beautiful mother
   with the baby in her arms.
They looked so very happy.
They made a beautiful picture.

The artist said,
  "I must make a picture
  of this beautiful mother."
He looked about him.
Soon he found the top
  of an old barrel.
It was big and round.
"Ho! Ho!" cried the artist,
  "Now I shall paint my picture!"

He began to draw.
He worked very fast.
He made all the lines go round
  like the circle.
See how mother tips her head
  to fit the circle!
See how the red sleeve curves
  just like the circle!
How the mother loves the baby!

Baby cuddles up to mother.
Mother puts her arm
    around the baby.
Baby's face is close
    to mother's face.
Baby's arm fits mother's arm.
See his pretty little feet!
They turn up
    just like the circle!

Little St. John is standing near.
He is a little shepherd boy.
He holds a little cross
    in his arms.
He folds his hands.
He looks up
    to the mother and child.
St. John loved the child Jesus
    and his beautiful mother.

37

The artist used many pretty colors
    in his picture.
The mother wears a red dress.
She has a blue robe
    on her lap.
She has a green shawl
    about her shoulders.
She wears a pretty cloth
    about her head.
Baby's dress is yellow.

The mother has big brown eyes.
She has soft brown hair.
She has a very gentle face.
Baby, too, has brown eyes.
He sits very, very still.
He sees far, far away.
Mother, baby, and St. John
    make a beautiful picture.

This is one of the great pictures
   of the world.
Today it hangs in a fine palace
   far across the sea.
Every day many people go
   to see this beautiful picture
   of Mother and Child.

THE STORY OF THE ARTIST

The artist is one
   of the greatest painters
   of the world.
His name is Raphael.

When Raphael was a little boy
   he learned to draw and paint.
His father was a painter.
His father taught him many things.

39

He taught him
  how to mix his colors.
He taught him
  how to use his brush.
He taught him many things
  about his paints and brushes!

Then Raphael grew to be a man.
He painted many pictures
  of a mother and her child.
One of these pictures he painted
  on the round top
  of an old barrel.

This is our picture
  of Mother and Child!
It is one
  of the most beautiful pictures
  in the whole world!

SOMETHING TO TELL

1. Who is the beautiful baby?
   Who is his little friend?

2. Why is it a round picture?
   Why does the mother tip her head?
   Why do baby's feet turn up?

3. What is the color
      of the Mother's dress?
   What is the color
      of baby's dress?

4. Why does St. John fold his hands?

5. What do you like best
   about the picture?

Related Music: LULLABY .... *Brahms*
                BABYLAND ...... *Pieine*

WITH GRANDMA

A visit to grandma!
How happy we are
  when we go to visit grandma!
She is so good and kind.
She tells us many happy stories.

One day a little girl
  went to visit her grandma.
She was a little Dutch girl.
She talked Dutch all the time.
Her grandma was Dutch, too.

In the picture she is sitting
  in the big chair.
She is a happy little girl.
She has a round face
  and yellow hair.

WITH GRANDMA
Budapest Gallery

ARTIST: Walter MacEwen
SCHOOL: American
DATES: 1860-1943

She wears a little cap
  such as all Dutch children wear.
She wears wooden shoes, too.
One shoe has come off.
It lies on the floor.

The little girl hugs her doll
  with one hand.
She puts the other hand on her hip.
She is thinking, as she listens
  to grandma's story.

How big and strong is grandma!
All Dutch grandmas are strong.
Grandma wears a cap, too.
It is tied under her chin.
Her brown dress has blue sleeves.
We can see grandma's strong arm.
Her arm is much stronger than baby's.

See grandma's face!
See baby's face!
Baby's skin is soft and fair.
Grandma's skin is brown.
Baby's cap is white.
Grandma's cap is dark.
Baby is such a little girl!
Grandma is so big and strong!

See the red cover on the table!
Is it like the color
  of baby's dress?
See the pitcher of water!
See the glass!
Baby may have a drink.
But baby does not want a drink!
She does not want to move.
She wants to sit very, very still
  and listen to her grandma.

Baby is so happy
  when she goes to visit grandma.
She does not want to go home.
No, no, no! She wants to stay
  with her good kind grandma!

Who can sit in a big chair
  as baby does?
You must hold a doll
  in your left hand.
You must put your right hand
  on your hip, just so.
You must let one shoe
  lie on the floor.
You must sit very, very still
  as you listen
  to all grandma says.
Who can sit in a big chair
  as baby does?

Who will be grandma?
She must be big and strong.
She must be good and kind.
She must sit
    beside her little Dutch girl.
Perhaps we can make a picture
    like our picture,—"With Grandma."

THE STORY OF THE ARTIST

This artist lived in America.
He went to Holland to paint.
There are many, many children
    in Holland!
He saw them playing
    on the sea shore.
He saw them sailing toy boats
    in the sea.
He painted many Dutch children!

One day the artist saw grandma
    with the little Dutch girl.
They sat so very still.
He said, "I must paint grandma
    and the little Dutch girl."
"O, do!" said the little Dutch girl,
    "I must have my picture
        with grandma!"
So the artist made this picture
    of the little Dutch girl
    with her grandma.
He painted
    baby's little round face
    and yellow hair.
He made grandma big and strong.
Then he said,
    "See my fine, new picture
    —'With Grandma'!"

SOMETHING TO TELL

1. Do you ever visit grandma?
Where does she live?

2. Where does this grandma live?
Who sits beside her?

3. What is grandma doing?
What does baby do?

4. What does baby hold in her hand?
What does she wear on her head?
What does she wear on her feet?

5. What is the color of baby's dress?
of grandma's dress?
Do you like baby and grandma?
Why?

Related Music: LIEBESFREUD..*Kreisler*
TRAUMEREI..*Schumann*

CHILDREN OF THE SHELL
Prado, Madrid

ARTIST: Bartolomé Esteban Murillo
SCHOOL: Spanish
DATES: 1616-1682

CHILDREN OF THE SHELL

See the beautiful children!
They are resting
 beside a little spring of water.
What a fine place
 for a cool fresh drink!

This is the child Jesus,
 and his playmate,
 the little Saint John.
All day long they have been at play.
They have had a fine time
 with the little white lamb.
Now they stop to rest
 beside the cool spring.

The spring is in a dark wood.
It is dark all about the spring.

See the happy smile
   upon the Christ-Child's face!
He holds the shell, full of water,
   for the little Saint John.
Little Saint John kneels.
He holds the shell, too,
   while he drinks.
The shell makes a fine cup.
It is such fun to drink
   from a shell!

The little white woolly lamb
   wants a drink, too.
Oh, yes! He sees the two children
   with the fresh cool water.
He raises his head.
He looks on
   while they drink.
Soon he will have some water.

Do you see the baby angels
  in the cloud above?
One, two, three!
Three beautiful baby angels
  in a cloud of light!

They see the happy children.
They see the little lamb.
They are happy baby angels.
They always watch
  over the Christ-Child
  and the little Saint John.

The Child must know
  the angels are near.
See! He raises his little hand.
Perhaps he is thinking about them.
Perhaps he is talking about them.
Do you think the Angels hear?

A beautiful golden light
  shines all around the angels.
It makes a great round circle.
It makes a circle of light
  about the Christ-Child's head.

The light shines
  on the two happy children.
It shines on the little pool
  of water.
It shines on the little lamb.
It makes a beautiful golden light
  in the dark wood.

Now we can see the two children!
We can see the little woolly lamb!
We can see the pretty shell.
We know why our picture is called,
    "Children of the Shell."

THE STORY OF THE ARTIST

This artist lived in sunny Spain
　　many, many years ago.
His name is Murillo.

When he was a little boy
　　he was very, very poor.
He grew to be
　　one of the greatest artists
　　in the whole world.

He loved to paint pictures
　　of children.
He painted little ragged children.
He painted little beggar children.
He painted many, many pictures
　　of the poor children
　　of Spain.

He painted the Christ-Child
   and the little Saint John
   many, many times.

Today these pictures
   are among the greatest pictures
   in the world.
They hang in a great palace
   far across the ocean
   in Spain.
The people of Spain
   are very proud
   of their beautiful pictures.
Every Sunday the people go
   to the palace
   to see Murillo's pictures.
They go often
   to see our beautiful picture,—
   "Children of the Shell."

SOMETHING TO TELL

1. Who are the two children?
   What are they doing?

2. What is the little lamb doing?

3. Who is watching
      over the children?

4. What makes the light?
   What is the color
      of the light?
   Where does it fall?

5. Why is our picture called,
      "Children of the Shell?"
   Do you like it? Why?

Related Music: BERCEUSE .....*Jarnefelt*
                         MELODY IN F..*Rubinstein*

PRINCESS MARGARITA THERESIA

See the little princess!
She is three years old.
She is having her picture painted.

What a proud little princess she is!
She is Princess Margarita Theresia.
She lived long ago in sunny Spain.
Her father was the king
    of Spain.
Her mother was the queen.

What a dear little princess she is!
She stands so very still.
She wears a beautiful dress
    of silk and lace.
See the pretty little skirt!
See the dark collar and cuffs!

PRINCESS MARGARITA THERESIA
Vienna Gallery

ARTIST: Don Rodriguez de Silva y Velasquez
SCHOOL: Spanish
DATES: 1599-1660

She holds a big fan
  in her little left hand.
She puts her right hand
  on the table.
She stands so very still
  as she looks
  at the artist
  while he paints.

See her pretty head!
See her pretty little face!
See her big, brown eyes!
She has a pretty little nose.
She has a pretty little mouth
  and pink cheeks.
She has pretty short hair, too.
She is such a dear little princess,—
  the little princess,
  Margarita Theresia!

The artist knew how to make
  a beautiful picture
  of the little princess.
He put many colors
  in her dress.
He put a vase of flowers
  on the table.
They are beautiful flowers.
Some are white, some are pink
  like the dress
  of the little princess.
The vase is dark
  like the collar and cuffs
  of the little princess.

The artist knew
  how to make
  a beautiful picture
  of the little baby princess.

On the floor he placed
  a very dark rug.
It, too, has pretty pink colors
  like the pink in the dress
  of the princess,
  only it is darker.

He put a dark green curtain
  at the back
  of the picture.
The curtain is very, very dark.
The princess is very, very light.
Now we can see her pretty dress
  of pink and gray
  against the dark green curtain!

The artist knew how to make
  a   beautiful picture
  of the little baby princess!

This little princess grew to be
  a very fine lady.
She had her picture painted
  many, many times.
But we like best of all
  her little baby picture
  when she was three years old.
She is such a dear little princess,—
  the little princess,
  Margarita Theresia!

THE STORY OF THE ARTIST

The artist lived
  in the king's palace.
He was the greatest painter
  in Spain.
He painted many pictures
  of the king and queen.

He painted many pictures
  of the king's children.
He painted many pictures
  of our little princess.

Margarita Theresia
  had a little brother.
His name was Don Carlos.
This artist painted many pictures
  of Don Carlos.
Some day you may see the picture
  of Don Carlos
  on his little chestnut pony.

The artist painted our picture
  of the little princess
  two hundred years ago.
It is one of the great pictures
  of the world.

SOMETHING TO TELL

1. Who is the little princess?
   Where did she live?

2. Who was her father?
   Who was her mother?

3. In what kind of house
   did they live?

4. Name the colors in her dress.
   Name the colors in the flowers.
   Name the colors in the rug.

5. Do you like the little princess?

Related Music:

TO A WILD ROSE....*MacDowell*

WALTZING DOLL ....*Poldini*

FEEDING HER BIRDS

One, two, three!
Three little children
  sitting in a row.
Mother called them.
They ran to the wide door-step.
Now they will have
  something good to eat.

One, two, three!
They sit in the wide door-way.
Sister holds her doll.
Brother sits
  between his little sisters.
Mother sits before them.
She feeds them
  as a mother bird
  feeds her baby birds.

FEEDING HER BIRDS
Lille Museum

ARTIST: Jean Francois Millet
SCHOOL: French
DATES: 1814-1875

The baby bird opens his mouth
  for the fat worm.
See little brother open his mouth
  for the warm broth!
He is just like a baby bird.

These little children
  live in France.
They wear wooden shoes.
See the round toes
  in the sunshine.
One, two, three, four, five, six!
Six little wooden shoes!

They wear light aprons
  and little caps.
Three light aprons, three little caps!
Mother wears a cap, too.
Mother's cap is blue.

See the old stone house!
It is a country house
   in France.
It is very, very old.
See the great stones
   in the door-way!

The door-step makes a fine seat
   for the little birds.
The stool makes a fine seat
   for the mother bird.
The vine makes green patches
   on the wall
   by the window.
There is green on the ground, too.

A big field
   lies back of the house.
Here father works all day long.

We see him
  through the open gate-way.
He looks so very small
  because he is so far away.

See the sunshine!
It lights up the wide door-way.
It lights up the faces
  of the little birds.
It lights up the end
  of the spoon.

Everybody looks at the spoon,—
  big sister, little sister,
  mother, and brother!
The hen comes running, too.
Cluck! Cluck! Cluck!
She thinks she will get a crumb.

The sun shines
   on the old stone house.
It lights up the wall.
It lights up the door-way.
See the warm, bright color
   of the stones!
They are yellow like sunlight.
But the sun shines brightest
   on the three little birds,
   on the mother bird,
   and on the end of the spoon.
Can you tell why?

The artist said his picture looked
   like a mother bird
   feeding her nest
   of baby birds.
So he called it
   "Feeding Her Birds."

THE STORY OF THE ARTIST.

This artist lived in France.
He lived far out
  in the country.
He knew all about the old houses
  of France.
He knew all about the children
  of France.
All his pictures tell
  of the country people
  of France.

He painted many
  of the great pictures
  of the world.
His name is Millet.
"Feeding Her Birds"
  is his picture
  that children like best.

SOMETHING TO TELL

1. Do you ever go to the country?

2. Where do these children live?
   What do they wear on their heads?
   What do they wear on their feet?

3. What is mother doing?
   Who gets the first spoonful? Why?
   Why does the hen come running?
   Where does everybody look?

4. Where is father?

5. What is the color of sunlight?
   Where is the sunlight brightest?
   Why did the artist call his picture
   "Feeding Her Birds"?

Related Music:

   MIGHTY LAK' A ROSE...*Nevin*

CHILDREN OF THE SEA

What fun it is
  to sail a toy boat in the sea!
What fun it is
  to let the wind carry it away!

These little children
  live in Holland.
They are Dutch children.
All day long they play
  in the sand.
They build sand houses.
They let the sea roll in
  and wash them all away.
They make toy boats.
They sail them in the sea.
Sometimes they make their boats
  of father's wooden shoes!

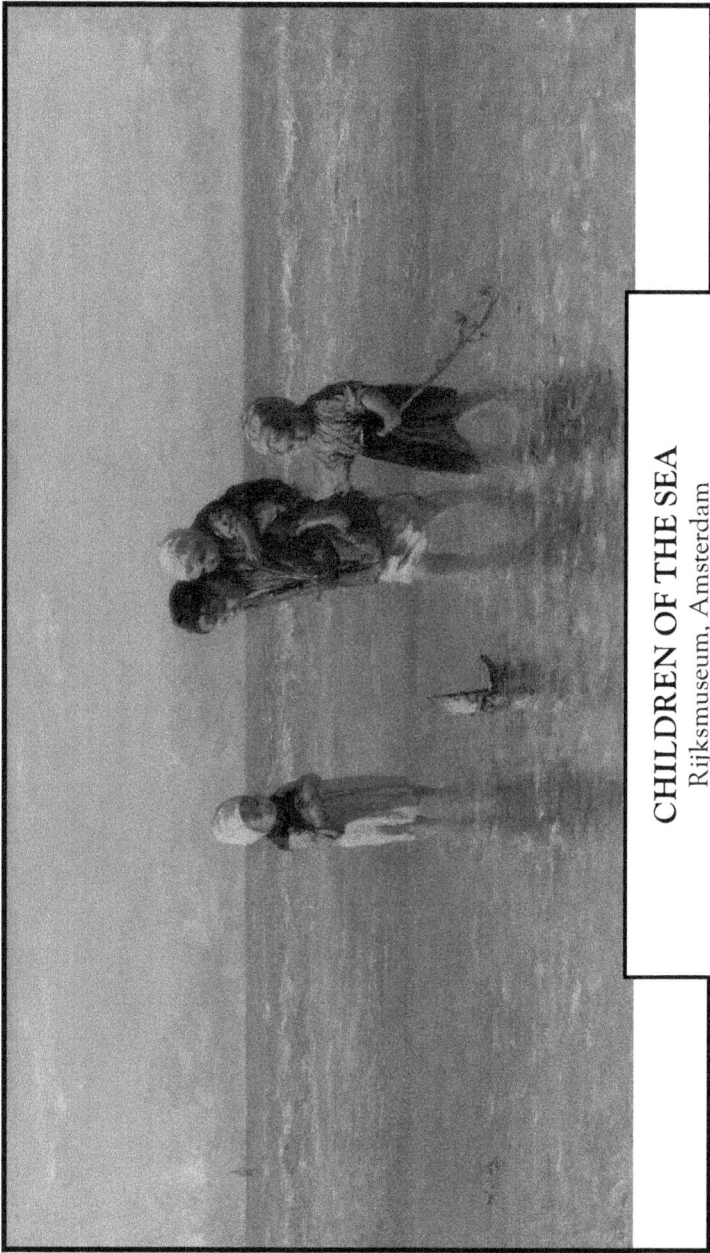

CHILDREN OF THE SEA
Rijksmuseum, Amsterdam

ARTIST: Josef Israels
SCHOOL: Dutch
DATES: 1824-1911

Big brother made this boat
   for his three little sisters.
He made the boat of wood.
He made the sail of white cloth.
Then it was ready to try.

Down to the sea they go!
Baby is too little
   to walk into the sea.
So big brother carries her
   on his back.
Into the water they go!

They set the little boat
   on the wave.
Soon the sail is full of wind.
One! Two! Three!
Off it goes!
Sail, sail away! Little boat!

Big brother is tallest.
He wears a dark cap.
Sisters wear little white caps.
All little girls in Holland
 wear white caps!
They wear wooden shoes.
What fun to live in Holland
 and wear wooden shoes!
What fun to live in Holland
 and sail toy boats
 in the sea!

How big the sea is!
It goes far, far out.
It goes as far
 as the eye can see.
There it meets the sky.
Do you see the boat
 away off on the water?

See the soft gray colors
　in the water!
Sometimes the sea is very blue.
Sometimes the sea is very green.
Sometimes the sun makes many colors
　in the sea.

How soft and gray the sky!
See the whitecaps rolling in!
They dance on the top
　of the waves.
The water is not deep
　near the shore
See the children's feet!
We can see how deep the water is!

The children
　watch their little boat.
Soon it will sail, sail away!

THE STORY OF THE ARTIST

This artist lived in Holland.
Holland is close to the sea.
Many of her streets are water.
They are called "canals."

Holland is the land
   of windmills.
Their great arms turn and turn.
Holland is the land
   of wooden shoes.
All the boys and girls
   wear tiny wooden shoes.
They go pat-a-pat, pat
   along the stony streets.

Every day the artist walked
   by the sea shore.
He saw the children at play.

He saw them sailing toy boats
in the sea.
He painted many pictures
of children by the sea.
"Children by the Sea"
is one of his best pictures.

Let us make a picture
of the sea,
of the big, blue sea!
We must place the skyline high.
Then it will be a big sea.
We must make the sky
soft and blue.
We must make the water
blue and green
with whitecaps.
Our boat must be a big boat.
Then it will sail, sail away.

SOMETHING TO TELL

1. Did you ever sail a boat?
   Where did you sail your boat?

2. Where do these children live?
   Where do they like to play?
   How do they make their boats?

3. How do you know the sea is big?
   Is it deep near the shore?
   Is it deep far out?

4. What is the color of the sea?
   What is the color of the sky?

5. What makes the whitecaps?
   What makes the little boat
   sail, sail away?

Related Music: PAPER BOATS . . . . *Sunne*
                 THE BOAT . . . . *Weidig*

HOLY NIGHT
Dresden Gallery

ARTIST: Antonio Allegri Correggio
SCHOOL: Italian
DATES: 1494-1534

HOLY NIGHT

It is Christmas eve.

It is night.

Far, far off, is the light
of early morning.

Shepherds are watching
their flocks by night.

The stars shine bright.

They hear the angels sing.

They are afraid.

Soon the angels lead them
to the place
where the young child lies.

See the wonderful picture!

It is full of light.

The light shines all about!

All the light comes
  from the Christ-Child.
It shines on the shepherds.
It shines on the angels above.
The light
  from the Christ-Child
  lights up the whole story.

The Christ-Child was born
  in a manger.
He lies upon the little straw bed.
The light shines all about him.

See the beautiful mother!
She looks down upon the child.
Her face is filled with light.
A woman stands near.
See her happy face!
The light shines all about her.

The shepherd boy looks up
  to the angels above.
There are so many angels!
They are singing beautiful songs.
The shepherd boy listens
  to the music.
His dog is beside him.
He sits very, very still.
He, too, sees the bright light.

The old shepherd has walked
  a long way.
He carries a heavy staff.
It has helped him
  over the hard ground.
Now he sees the bright light!
How it shines on his face!
He raises his hand in wonder.
He gazes at the Christ-Child!

The light shines
   on all the pretty colors.
See the mother's soft blue dress!
It is filled with light.
See the little straw bed.
It is golden yellow.
See the white fleecy clouds
   as they float above!
See the angels' pretty colors
   of red and green!

Outside, all is dark.
It is night.
Far, far off is the light
   of early morning.
See the father with the donkey
   standing near!
He hears the angels sing!
He sees the shining light!

Inside, all is light.
The mother is happy!
The angels sing!
They know it is the birth-day
 of the Christ-Child!

RING OUT, CHRISTMAS BELLS!
FOR YOUR GLAD SONG TELLS
"THE CHRIST-CHILD IS BORN
 TODAY!"

THE STORY OF THE ARTIST

Many, many years ago,
 there lived a great painter.
His name was Correggio.
He lived far, far
 across the ocean.
He painted many, many pictures.
He loved to paint light.

He filled his pictures
   with bright, beautiful light.
This made them shine
   even in darkness.

Correggio is the painter of LIGHT.
He painted our picture, "Holy Night,"
   three hundred years ago.
This is his greatest picture.
Today it hangs
   in a beautiful palace
   far across the sea.
Many, many people go
   to the palace every day
   to see the beautiful picture.
It is one of the greatest pictures
   in the whole world.
The LIGHT makes it beautiful.

SOMETHING TO TELL

1. Why do we celebrate Christmas?
   When does Christmas come?

2. What story does the picture tell?
   Who is the Baby?

3. What makes the great light?
   Where does it shine brightest?
   Who are standing near?

4. Why is it dark outside?

5. What do you see above?
   Is there music in the picture?
   Where?
   What does this artist paint best?

Related Music:

ADESTE FIDELES—Portugal...
SILENT NIGHT ....*Gruber*
THE FIRST NOËL..(*Traditional*)

PRONUNCIATION OF PROPER NAMES

CALMADY .... (kăl' mă dĭ)

CORREGGIO .... (kō rĕd' jō)

HALS .... (halz)

MACEWEN .... (măc ū' ĕn)

MILLET .... (mē' yā')

MURILLO .... (mōō rē' lyō)

RAPHAEL .... (rä' fā ĕl)

VAN DYCK .... (văn dīk')

VELASQUEZ ..... (vā läs' kăth)

SUGGESTIONS TO TEACHERS

STUDYING THE PICTURE. Any picture presented for study becomes more interesting when freely discussed in a natural way by the class. Before reading the text it is always advisable to study the picture. Pupils should be encouraged to give their own impressions; tell what they like in a picture, and WHY they like it.

In the primary grades the story interest is uppermost,—"what is it all about?" By tactful questioning the teacher may bring out many artistic points for observation. She may speak of color and action as well as story content. She may lead the pupils to discover new words which will appear in the text. These may be emphasized, written upon the board and studied. Thus they are greeted like old friends when met in the story.

DRAMATIZATION. In the primary grades many pictures lend themselves to dramatization. With little children the "acting out" of the picture is a real joy. Under no circumstances is it necessary to burden oneself with an EXACT reproduction in the class room. The details of costume are not required. Any outstanding accessory, however, easily at hand, may add interest. It is the EFFORT on the part of the child to reproduce the pose and action that is of value. Frequently, if time permits, children may take turns in posing letting the class decide who does best. Thus in a simple and direct way, many of the pictures selected for primary study may be given an added interest and charm.

CORRELATION. Language lessons both oral and written may be based on the work in picture-study. The questions following each picture, when answered either orally or in written form, necessitate close observation and intelligent expression.

As far as possible, each child should own his own pictures. This leads to the making of picture-study books, envelopes, folders, calendars, and other simple projects which utilize and also preserve the pictures.

The music hour offers still another opportunity for related study. Pictures, like music, create emotions. When possible in the study of pictures, add the music which may suggest the spirit and atmosphere of the picture. THE INTEREST IS ALWAYS KEENLY STIMULATED WHEN PORTIONS FROM VARIOUS SELECTIONS ARE PLAYED, AND THE CHILDREN PERMITTED TO CHOOSE THE ONE BEST SUITED TO THE PICTURE.

The suggestions for musical selections which follow the questions on the picture will be of great value to the teacher.

To be introduced in the early years to the masterpieces of the ages, and to learn of the kingly minds who have ruled in this realm of beauty, is sure to develop an interest which will enlarge, enrich and refine the future life of the pupil.

www.ingramcontent.com/pod-product-compliance
Lightning Source LLC
LaVergne TN
LVHW010310070426
835511LV00021B/3459